COLONIAL HOMES

Verna Fisher

Nomad Press
A division of Nomad Communications
10 9 8 7 6 5 4 3 2 1

This book was manufactured by
Regal Printing Limited in China
June 2010, Job #1005018
ISBN: 978-1-934670-98-9

Illustrations by Andrew Christensen

Questions regarding the ordering of this book should be addressed to
Independent Publishers Group
814 N. Franklin St.
Chicago, IL 60610
www.ipgbook.com

Nomad Press
2456 Christian St.
White River Junction, VT 05001
www.nomadpress.net

Contents

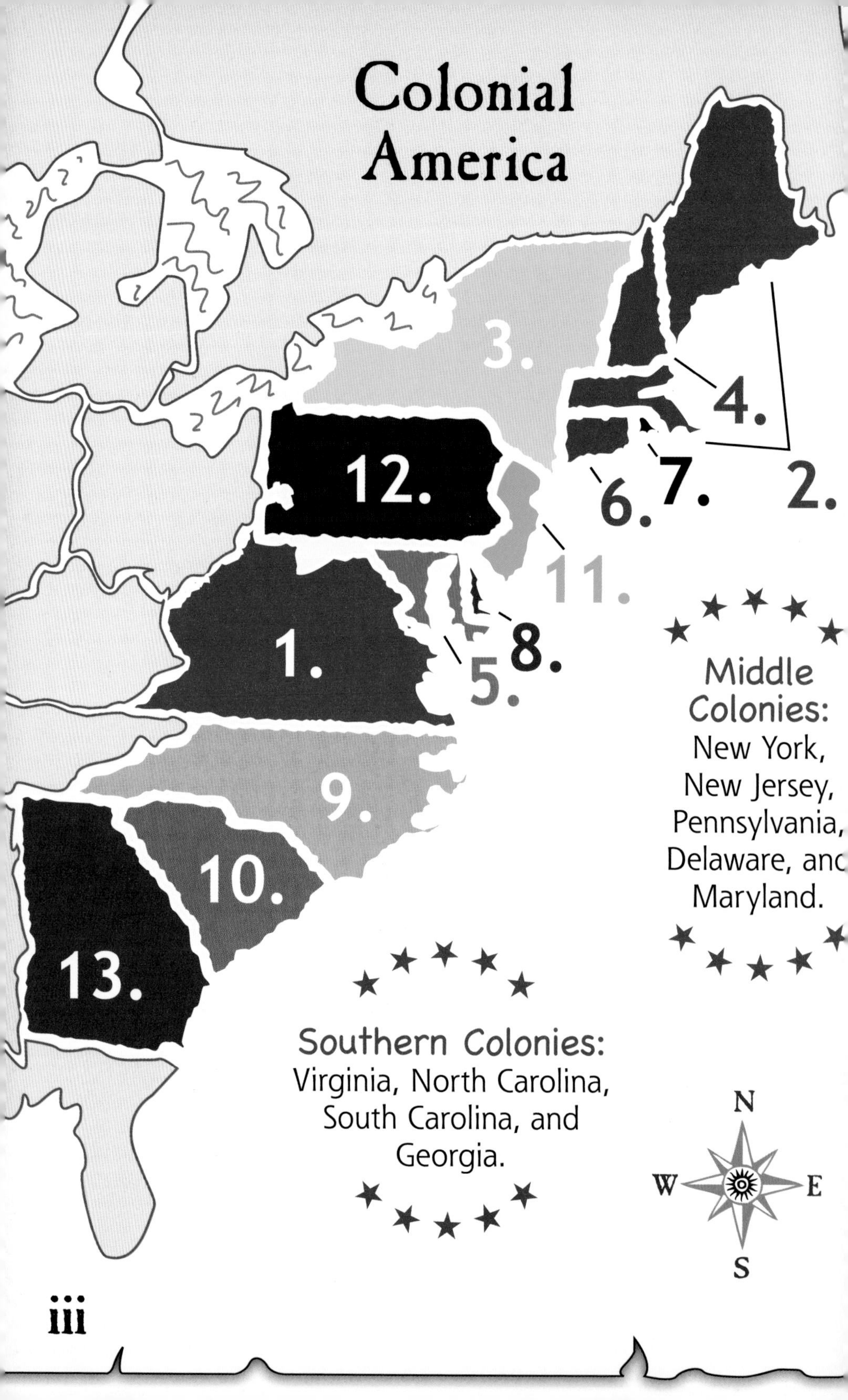
Colonial America
3.
4.
12.
6.
7.
2.
11.
1.
8.
5.
9.
10.
13.
Middle Colonies:
New York,
New Jersey,
Pennsylvania,
Delaware, and
Maryland.
Southern Colonies:
Virginia, North Carolina,
South Carolina, and
Georgia.
N
W
E
S

★ ★ ★ ★ ★

New England:
Massachusetts,
New Hampshire, Connecticut,
and Rhode Island.

In the 1600s, people began leaving Europe to settle in America. Some were explorers searching for gold, while others came looking for freedom.

Jamestown in Virginia and Plymouth in Massachusetts were two of the earliest settlements where these people came to start a new life.

1607

1. **Virginia**
2. **Massachusetts**
3. **New York**
4. **New Hampshire**
5. **Maryland**
6. **Connecticut**
7. **Rhode Island**
8. **Delaware**
9. **North Carolina**
10. **South Carolina**
11. **New Jersey**
12. **Pennsylvania**
13. **Georgia**

1733

A New World

The first **colonists** in America came from England. To get to the **New World**, they had to travel by ship for many weeks.

When they finally reached land, they must have been very happy, but also very tired and hungry. Most importantly, they needed **shelter**!

Words to Know

colonist: a person who came to settle America.

New World: what is now America. It was called the New World by people from Europe because it was new to them.

shelter: a place to live that protects a person from the weather.

wilderness: land that is not settled or changed by people.

When the colonists arrived, most of the land in America was forest and **wilderness**. There were no towns or roads like the ones the colonists had left behind in Europe.

The First Colonial Homes at Jamestown

In 1607, a group of English colonists built a settlement in Jamestown, Virginia. Unfortunately, the colonists were not very prepared for this project. Many did not know the first thing about building a house. They also did not have the right tools.

Words to Know

colony: early settlement in America.

Did You Know?

Jamestown was the first permanent English colony. The colonists faced disease and often did not get along with their Native American neighbors. There was not enough food. Although many colonists died, the colony was still able to survive and grow.

So, what did the colonists do? They made the best shelter they could, with the supplies that they had. Some may have made a kind of tent at first, while others were able to build small, one-room homes.

A **colony** settled nearby at Roanoke in 1587 did not survive. It is still a mystery what happened to the people of Roanoke. Roanoke is called the Lost Colony.

In Massachusetts, the first colonists built into the sides of hills to make their huts strong.

The first homes at Jamestown were made from **wattle** and **daub**. The colonists cut trees for logs, and carved **posts** and **beams** from the logs.

After standing the posts up, they wove branches and sticks between them and stuffed the spaces with straw. This was the wattle.

wattle: sticks and straw filling the spaces between posts.

daub: clay mixture used to cover the wattle in between posts of colonial houses.

post: a strong piece of wood standing up straight for support.

beam: a strong piece of wood laid across the posts for support.

thatch: straw used to make a roof.

Words to Know

Then the colonists covered the wattle with a clay mixture, called daub. The daub kept out wind, water, and animals. Finally, the colonists used the beams to make the roof. They covered the roof with **thatch**.

Different Types of

Across **Colonial America**, the colonists built different types of homes. People from Ireland, Scotland, Germany, and Sweden built log cabins. These homes were made of rounded logs stacked on top of each other.

Colonial Homes

Words to Know

Colonial America:
the name given to America when talking about the years 1607–1776.

Log cabins were very popular because they could be built quickly and didn't use any nails. Metal for nails was expensive and not always available.

Words to Know

notch: a V-shaped cut.

chink: stuffing the spaces between logs with small pieces of wood.

paneling: thin, smooth, flat pieces of wood.

Then and Now

In colonial times there was no electricity. It hadn't been invented yet. The colonists used candles for light in the evening.

Today we have electric lights so we can see when it gets dark. All we have to do is flip the switch.

How did the logs stay in place? The logs had **notches** cut at their ends. They locked into place at their corners when they were stacked together.

The colonists **chinked** the space between the logs with pieces of wood, then smeared daub over it. Sometimes they covered the dirt floor and rough log walls of the cabins with **paneling**.

Building a house was hard work. The colonists often built homes together. Kids also helped out. Building a house was a community effort!

Can you imagine life without electricity? That means no TV, no computers, no telephones, no refrigerators, no hot water from the tap.

If you had been alive then, what job would you have liked to do? Cut the trees down for logs? Mix up some daub to fill in the cracks?

Native American Homes

Of course, the colonists weren't the only people living in Colonial America! Native Americans had lived in the New World for thousands of years.

Here and There

In Native American villages the houses were very close to each other. They were not separated by yards or streets.

In colonial villages, houses were separated by yards and streets.

Native Americans lived their lives according to the seasons. During the spring, summer, and fall, they often moved to different areas to fish or hunt. They might gather fruits that were coming into season. After gathering enough food for the winter, the Native Americans would move back to their winter villages.

There were many styles of Native American homes. The style depended on where the **tribe** lived. When we think of Native American homes, we usually think of tipis. A tipi is similar to a tent because it is built from poles and enclosed by a covering.

Most tipis were covered with either thin layers of bark from a tree or animal skins. They could be rolled up and moved easily when the village needed to move to an area with more food.

Tipis were used by tribes living in the western part of America.

Words to Know

tribe: a large group of people with common ancestors and customs.

Longhouses were another type of Native American home. These were **oblong**-shaped houses shared by several families. Longhouses were covered with wide sheets of bark. These homes were most common along the East Coast, and often used by the **Iroquois** people.

A typical longhouse might have enough room for 10 families, with around 60 people able to fit inside. Larger longhouses could hold over 150 people, but they were less common.

Each family had its own sleeping and cooking area in the longhouse.

oblong: a stretched-out rectangle with round corners.

Iroquois: a group of Native American tribes that lived in what is now New York and Canada.

Words to Know

Other Native Americans lived in **wigwams**. These round houses were made of bark sheets stretched over poles into a dome shape. The ground acted as the floor.

Wigwams were smaller than longhouses, and designed just for one family. They were common among the northern **Algonquian**-speaking tribes. Because wigwams could be built quickly and made good shelters, they were popular.

wigwam: a dome-shaped house made with bark covering a frame of saplings.

Algonquian: a group of tribes that lived in Canada and America, east of the Rocky Mountains. They spoke languages that were related.

Words to Know

Changes in Colonial Homes Over Time

Early colonial homes were one-room **cottages**. A large fireplace provided heat for the house, as well as a place to cook food. The homes did not have a lot of furniture, because the settlers didn't have time to make it.

Words to Know

ottage: a small house, usually
nly one story tall.

edstead: the framework
a bed, which supports
e mattress.

At first, the settlers slept on the floor on mattresses filled with straw. Later, they built bedframes called **bedsteads**. Wealthy colonists slept on mattresses filled with feathers.

As time went by, the colonists were able to build larger houses, or add on to their old homes to make them bigger. By the 1700s, some of the new houses were pretty fancy. Many had an upper floor with several bedrooms.

Some people owned brick houses. Many had large porches, also known as verandas. Sometimes, these verandas were enclosed porches on the upper levels of houses.

Did You Know?

Most colonial children had to share a bed with their brothers and sisters. They often slept in a trundlebed, a low bed that rolled out from under another bed.

You can still see these beautiful colonial houses in many towns in the original 13 colonies.

Glossary

Algonquian: a group of tribes that lived in Canada and America, east of the Rocky Mountains. They spoke languages that were related.

beam: a strong piece of wood laid across the posts for support.

bedstead: the framework of a bed, which supports the mattress.

cottage: a small house, usually only one story tall.

chink: stuffing the spaces between logs with small pieces of wood.

Colonial America: the name given to America when talking about the years 1607–1776.

colony: early settlement in America.

colonist: a person who came to settle America.

daub: clay mixture used to cover the wattle in between posts of colonial houses.

Iroquois: a group of Native American tribes that lived in what is now New York and Canada.

longhouse: an oblong-shaped house shared by many families.

New World: what is now America. It was called the New World by people from Europe because it was new to them.

notch: a V-shaped cut.

oblong: a stretched-out rectangle with round corners.

paneling: thin, smooth, flat pieces of wood.

post: a strong piece of wood standing up straight for support.

shelter: a place to live that protects a person from the weather.

thatch: straw for a roof.

tipi: a house similar to a tent, with upright poles covered by animal skins.

tribe: a large group of people with common ancestors and customs.

trundlebed: a low bed pushed under another bed when not in use.

wattle: sticks and straw filling the spaces between posts.

wigwam: a dome-shaped house made with bark covering a frame of saplings.

wilderness: land that is not settled or changed by people.

Further Investigations

Books

Bordessa, Kris. *Great Colonial America Projects You Can Build Yourself.* White River Junction, VT: Nomad Press, 2006.

Fisher, Verna. *Explore Colonial America! 25 Great Projects, Activities, Experiments.* White River Junction, VT: Nomad Press, 2009.

Museums and Websites

Colonial Williamsburg
www.history.org
Williamsburg, Virginia

National Museum of the American Indian
www.nmai.si.edu
Washington, D.C. and New York, New York

Plimoth Plantation
www.plimoth.org
Plymouth, Massachusetts

America's Library
www.americaslibrary.gov

Jamestown Settlement
www.historyisfun.org

Native American History
www.bigorrin.org

Native Languages of the Americas
www.native-languages.org

Social Studies for Kids
www.socialstudiesforkids.com

The Mayflower
www.mayflowerhistory.com

Virtual Jamestown
www.virtualjamestown.org

Index